BUTTERFLIES AT HOPE STATION

Selected Poems by
Suzi Rapoport

Blue Magnolia Press

Butterflies at Hope Station
ISBN 978-1-3999-7400-4

Published by Blue Magnolia Press

Blue Magnolia Press
London
UK

Copyright © Suzi Rapoport 2024
www.suzirapoport.com

Edited by Rohan Quine
Cover artwork by Suzi Rapoport
Cover design by Vinko Kalcic
Author cover photo by Craig Revel Horwood
Logo design & interior layout by Clifford Leo Harris
@clixxord

All other creatures look down toward the earth, but man was given a face so that he might turn his eyes toward the stars and his gaze upon the sky.

—Ovid, *Metamorphoses*

Poetry is not an end in itself out in the service of life; of what use are poems, or any other works of art, unless to enable human lives to be lived with insight of a deeper kind…

—Kathleen Raine

Foreword

It is with supreme delight and heartfelt joy that I introduce you to this exquisite collection of poetry by my dear friend of many years, Suzi Rapoport. I am filled with an irresistible sense of privilege to present the talent of such a gifted writer.

Within the pages of this amazing collection of work, you'll venture into a beguiling journey through the realms of emotion, where every verse serves as a window into the depths of the author's soul.

Suzi's words are carefully woven with the graceful strokes of a poet's brush. Her words transport you to captivating worlds, where dreams dance with reality.

Each poem is permeated with profound meaning, inviting the reader to explore the rich tapestry of life. Through a dazzling dance of metaphor and imagery, Suzi ensnares the nature of life's joys and sorrows, its triumphs and tribulations, with an exceptional authenticity that will echo profoundly within one's heart.

What sets this fabulous work apart is the impressive ability of Suzi to fluently craft verses that transcend the boundaries of time and space. With her words, Suzi creates a parallel universe where one can find condolence and cheer, inspiration and understanding.

I encourage you to read these verses not just as words on a page but as a penetrating connection between kindred spirits. Be transported, to feel profoundly and to hug the gorgeousness that lies between the lines. You'll soon discover Suzi's collection is not only a reflection of her voice, but an invitation to discover your own.

—Craig Revel Horwood, *Strictly Come Dancing* judge, theatre director, autobiographer and novelist.

Introduction

It all began with a dream I had as a child. I entered the mouth of a whale, sat down for a meal at a table in its stomach, then tiptoed into a gallery, looking in wonder at the paintings, before stepping into the sea.

I wrote the dream down; it became a poem … and since then, the poems haven't stopped. That child believed in herself with an innocence that led her to recite her poetry at bus stops.

This volume, *Butterflies at Hope Station*, is a home for a sequence of poems drawn from across my own span of life —a cascade of water from the same waterfall.

—Suzi Rapoport

Contents

Butterflies at Hope Station	13
Gift	14
Water-framed	15
Mermaid	16
Rhythm	17
Unforeseen	18
Shade of My Lipstick	19
Green Slithery Moss	20
Back to Back	22
Two Serpents	23
Kitchen on the Mend	24
Talking to My Soap	25
Restaurant Table	26
Balloon	27
Muddle	28
Blue Mauve Station	29
New Blue Places	30
Expectation	31
Gladioli and Violets	32
Kaleidoscope	33
Attraction	34
A Kiss in Time	35

Taken and Enjoyed	36
Radiance	37
It's Late	38
Identity	39
Too Much Too Soon	40
Misinformed	41
A Fine Way to Wake up	42
Open and Shut	43
After the Picnic	44
Ideal	45
Good Reason	46
Query	47
Duck Farm	48
Honey Spirit	49
Heat	50
Many Years Later	51
Provides Merriment	52
Echo	53
Him and That Party	54
Buried in the Night	56
Infinity	57
Meadows	58

Butterflies at Hope Station

I take a train to leave my mood behind.
The doors shut it out.

Three stations on, a sailor salutes me.
Bending forward, his basket of butterflies
sprays itself into the sun.

A perfumed cloud descends.
Hope comes to visit.

Gift

He came in, unexpected,
on a winter-filled night.
While lovers caressed,
he came in, grinning.

    "I'll make you my package," she thought,
    "you will be my eternal
    Christmas and birthday gift!"

        She loved her parcel.
        Even after she'd opened it,
        knowing the contents but still unable
        to solve its mystery.

            Later on
            she took his fingers
            between the notes of her lips—
            and the music was spectacular.

Water-framed

Frozen pipes create cold havoc;
a hanging cottage near collapse
provides the setting we need.

No anchor tying us down
alarms me, though…

Slush of water, pleasing our feet.

Mermaid

She leans over the sea,
watching dreams swirl over her body.

Roaming sea-gardens,
placing silence
into water.

She laughs aloud at the world
with all its creases, and returns
to where shells lie at her feet.

Rhythm

Your words draw curtains,
create soft shades.

Into this cold room
you pulsate.

Unforeseen

She came to see him.

He stood in his doorway.
Lean. Full lips.

She arrived anxious,
soft speech sliding…

He felt himself
flounder
in her slipstream.

Shade of My Lipstick

I'll darken the shade of my lipstick for you.
I'll darken the shades of my moods, if you'd like.

Your face masks our evening,
the mystery of Halloween
and all the skies' candles.

Listening to an unusual concert,
our breezy talk develops.

Seven wishes make life pleasurable,
when we lie in the bedroom's diffused light,
when we don't need to speak to each other.

Total acceptance delights.

Leaning to where the sky breaks
into patterns,
I detect hope.

Green Slithery Moss

Slushy,
splashy,
hot and
slashy.
Gooey,
sickly,
thick and
messy.

Let us put our feet into it,
let us roll and jump onto it,
let us laugh loud and clear,
let us cry soft warm tears.

Slushy,
splashy,
hot and
slashy.
Gooey,
sickly,
thick and
messy.

Let us dance, sing and shout,
let us dip our toes in deep,
let us throw ourselves about,
let us feel its smearing heat.

Slushy,
splashy,
hot and
slashy.
Gooey,
sickly,
thick and
messy.

Let us go home covered in dirt,
let us sing pretty songs on the way,
let us say we've been at work,
let us think it's been a glorious day.

Back to Back

I took my courage out for a walk.
It began to knock me on the head,
displayed a fighting mood
and pointed out my weaknesses.

I told my courage: settle down.
It merely turned itself around.
Then both of us sat on a friendly bank:
sitting that way, back to back.

Two Serpents

One had eyes full of treachery;
the other, mysterious eyes.

One had the eyes of a tyrant;
the other, a serpent's wisdom.

He danced so well with him,
the one felt the other's breath
loosening his
limbs.

Kitchen on the Mend

My kitchen has suffered a heart attack.
Too much activity has spoiled its harmony.

I make ridiculous mistakes.
A frozen product still needs to be thawed.
Bottles knock against my hand,
producing sudden bruises.

Yet a need to express bright colour
in a paradise of cookery ads
tempts me to delights,
and all the supermarket's brightly-coloured wrappings
have come to visit.
Bamboo straw containers take refreshment
under vibrant vegetables;
shiny pots, steamers re-dance their former cadences.

In the kitchen a radio plays,
in the kitchen with its mantelpiece
of pickling jars.

Many well-known plumbers
have left cards in my letter-box.
How lucky that my taps are working.
My stove is in order.
My kitchen is recovering.

Talking to My Soap

There are no half-hung pieces of laundry on my line,
there is no dirt.

I know you think that soap in the kitchen
should be the liquid sort
and there's nothing else as good.

Afternoon frustration,
straw hats squashed—
ah but that rhubarb is beautiful.

No matter what your mirror says,
you are only a product,
same as the soap. But I'll not package you—
though you insist I be boxed.

Restaurant Table

I am being surveyed,
lips to heart.

His being flatters.

Here I am
on the opposite side.

He stays silent
while chatter continues.

He is all observation.

Despite his avoidance,
I am scattered and amazed.

Balloon

My smile flies from my face
like a balloon let loose,
floating through the air.

Muddle

No bells on his toes.
No telephone to say
can you help me mother?
Why, heaven help the goldfish on a
night like this,
swimming round and round.

Walking down the street, a bag of
flour fell out of her basket.
Went to help her.
"Do not bother, it's self-raising,"
she said.

A deaf and dumb person goes into a
shop, gesticulates for a saw.
A blind man does the same. What does he do?
He asks for it.

Blue Mauve Station

Blue mauve railway station.
Someone whistles—
just another reaction.

Blue soft grey
the embrace between us,
foggy and calm.

Your voice has risen
an octave:
pips and peels of laughter
bouncing back to me.

New Blue Places

Kiss, kiss,
sweet bliss;
racing to new places.

Many things to do,
absolutely true,
nothing works
unless I have you.
Hello, Mr. Dedicated
to keeping things new.

Mr. True,
sometimes you're also
my little blue love,
through and through.

Expectation

She came with hope, and then
what she had hoped for had gone;
so she left.

And then the thing for which she had hoped
arrived.

Gladioli and Violets

At a flower stall where George sells
his orchids and lilies, he confesses
he doesn't like flowers
except for gladioli.
Stems reach from below
as each bud swells.

George tells me of a man he knew
years ago,
who went selling violets
until the butcher complained
about the distracting smell.

Before we part, George reaches to get me
some carnations that have fallen loose.
Enclosed in folds of paper, they
see me through the afternoon.

Kaleidoscope

I place us into a bag
and shake it.

I put our love and hope in there.

Juggling all my thoughts of you,
I make my evening into a party.

Attraction

What is it about him
that startles me every time we speak?
The muse starts playing tricks—
I am spirited away.

When he smiles
my toes tingle.

A Kiss in Time

At first he panics,
then the blend
of unexpected harmony
reaches through to him.

At last
he feels unthreatened;
she reciprocates …
means only
to touch his existence,
very delicately.

Taken and Enjoyed

Travelling through your eyes …
our pupils reflect
an absoluteness
that has been a lantern
since we met.

Too tired to walk back to your home,
we spend our first night
in a rose-pillowcased room.

Taken and enjoyed, absorbing
a potpourri of linked scents,
your kisses sailing fresh,
our fluency and fingers
trace our meeting into place.

Radiance

People magnified ten thousand times
travel towards bright stars,
spinning into glory,
radiating smiles.

Our lives bear stretch-marks
from which beauty reels.

It's Late

While you lie next door in my heart,
I need to go where you are,
hold you in my arms, although we both know
our love has ended.

Feeling sad,
wanting to be held by you again,
while pride drills resentment deep inside.

It's late, I need no stranger's arms,
but yours, around me.

Outside, the cars are silent.

Identity

I reciprocate with anything.
I am here to reciprocate.
I'm on fire. I am truth:
I don't flick ash on your carpets.

I am the tap of genius.
I'm suspicion where envy has rooted itself.
I am snake—
poisonous cobra of immortality.

I am nakedness of fear.

Too Much Too Soon

This love thing
is not what I intended.

When he gets into bed
I am fed up with him.

There is too much bliss
in his kissing.

Misinformed

You talk about computerising people
in an over-populated world.
Let's schedule existence
by aleatoric operations.
A hole in the head, chip surgery.
That way, planes fly according to plan.

"I don't know," I say. "I don't fly planes."

You say it's the rage
to be operated on.
The pilot is a computer.
"I know," you say. "I am the big dealer."

My mouth wide open,
don't drip any chips in it,
your face is iron, your words are steel;
what you say is credible,
incredibly warped yet real.

I shudder.

A Fine Way to Wake up

Six months of travelling towards
a fake expression.
His features
only fine because she
decided he would be that way.

Six months of travelling nowhere.
After long enough his lack of warmth
shook her in every nerve.

Six months of travelling nowhere.
A fine way to wake up.

Open and Shut

Doors open, doors shut
in my mind, as it explores time.
Pulled like a puppet
on the strings of fate.

Once I was too late;
now I stand, not knowing
which door to take.

You asked me to visit,
when I was about to leave.
I didn't ask entry
at the beginning.

I awoke from a sad dream.
What depressed me
was the man who left
through the half-open door.

After the Picnic

Sometimes I go out
with a picnic basket.
I wonder if I will find you
by the wayside,
your bottled-up thoughts
suspended.

I don't want to live with a
tin of dead tomato soup.

Ideal

He has not yet appeared,
a bright knight on a white charger.

Yet the charge of my adrenaline
returns me to those days of chivalry.

Good Reason

If only one could say
it was this or it was that.
There were doubtless reasons
they split up.

Instead, she reframes the emotional
transformation
as self-survival.

It surely will be kinder
for them both
on the empty road
without each other.

Query

If I could look into dark
and from dark find light;
no frightening staircase
facing the turned-out light …
I could find the way to hope
across pain's troubled nerves.

Duck Farm

It all began at a party.
Challenged by the host to quack,
she accepted—
quacked back.

Waddling along…

A year later,
on their farm,
      quack … quack
                quack … quack
                          quack … quack.

Honey Spirit

Spirit of the Muse,
you weren't long in persuading me
to follow you.
See the trapeze artist,
he understands your call
as he masquerades,
unsurpassable.

Muse, you delight me,
I know myself to be
The pollen for my own pursuit.
I am a honeypot, too—golden.

Heat

He brings the kitchen to life—
dishes colour the counter.

I await his movements,
which change
the composition of the room.

In responding to him,
celluloid transfers itself,
transparency is tangible.

His stunning eyes.

Many Years Later

His hands weave through her senses,
his eyes glow
with a translucent energy
within them both
still alive
and flowing.

Provides Merriment

He calculated the length of his kisses.
He gave more than he needed to receive.

Life opens out through their winter setting,
sun dazzles body union,
beneath sheets
love speaks,
life teases,
pricks
senses usually hidden.

Echo

My voice is reaching an expression,
a suggestion
mirrored in a flower.

Him and That Party

They meet at a party
where the people unsettle her mood.
He brings her to life.

In the tree's dark morning chorus,
tenuous winter light.

Each time he approaches,
her trembling
revives their night.
He moves generously.
His timing
skips on air.
Dancers in their love's ballet.

Country air calls them out,
arms open wide,
two gates ahead.

Later alone, she walks in his garden.
Thorn bushes cling to her.
A statue sits on his frozen pond,
still frowning,
as it must have done through his childhood.

Here are paths
crossing hills
where he walked
years ago.

She has traced his routes now,
back to that bedroom
with its wallpaper
covered in those ladies and those gentlemen—
turn of the century.

Buried in the Night

This is where he once said, "The room is dark, too dim for us,
how can we make love without light?"
Turned on every switch, pulled the curtains open.
They didn't stop all day.

The flowers smell of everything forgotten.

They bury her in the evening.
It was tantalising to return to this room.
But her memory haunts him.
He shouldn't have come back.

Infinity

Our friendly fingers
are garlands.
Newness brightens the night
where they circle,
accepting space.

You're there, I'm here.
Between us lies infinity.

Meadows

I feel my heart tip-toeing over,
and hope I never fall.

Not daring to disclose my love,
wondering how much you know.

Your hands make petals of my arms,
your eyes induce a somersault of hope!
Our lives fall into place
as easily as meadows fit together.

About the Author

Suzi is an artist and poet who lives in London. She has fed her creativity travelling throughout the world, where along the way she spent time living in Antibes, in Sydney, and the longest spell in the Hollywood Hills. It was here where modelling work, "hanging-out" and much spontaneous partying were balanced with days of spiritual and creative solitude on a terrace perched high above Woodrow Wilson Drive, reading or writing her poems and journals.

It was in Los Angeles that she gave some of her earliest poetry readings. Suzi has since performed internationally including in London, the U.S. and New Zealand, with James Ragan, Alan Brownjohn, Jeremy Reed, Michael Horowitz, Alexis Lykiard, Labi Siffre and many others.

On returning to the UK she began a long association with the anti-establishment literary periodical *Ambit*. Her poems have appeared alongside the works of a range of esteemed writers and artists including Stevie Smith, Peter Porter, Carol Ann Duffy, Fleur Adcock, Eduardo Paolozzi and Peter Blake.

With a life story that should be a book in itself, one of the achievements of which she is most proud is the securing of a plaque for her friend Hugo Manning, poet, mystic and former poetry editor of *The New Statesman*. The plaque, created by the sculptor David McFall, was mounted in 1982 on the façade of Manning's last home.

In addition to poetry and some of the beautiful people with whom she's shared adventures over the years, Suzi's other great love is painting and she has exhibited at a number of venues across London. She continues to create in both artforms and intends to never stop doing so.

Suzi Rapoport's collection of poetry, *Butterflies at Hope Station*, is a passionate chronicle of a life well lived. Her poems are rays of light illuminating hope in the shadowed memory of joyful mysteries. Whether "placing silence into water" or hearing "soft speech sliding", her voice is one of enriched generosity, dancing language through a world in need of her calming spirit. Her poetry radiates in the mind's space of imagination like slides of photographs projected on a drifting cloud.

—James Ragan, poet, playwright, screenwriter and educator

Suzi's poems shimmer. Vivid, thoughtful scenes that explode into the fantastic and colourful. Every one is a kaleidoscopic gem.

—Phil Wang, comedian and author

Butterflies at Hope Station traverses time, and in the most nimble manner, through her poetry and choice of words. Suzi has distilled a life's fleeting moments of passion and despair into a guilty pleasure. Once in this seductive world you will share at her table and be left craving more. A real triumph.

—Amanda Watt, painter

A collection of impressionistic snapshots. If Renoir had written poetry it might have come out like this. That said, beneath Suzi Rapoport's butterfly clouds there's a beady-eyed consciousness at work. If you're going to Hope Station, expect to have your ticket inspected.

—Ian Pattison, TV writer and novelist

From poem to poem or from line to line, sensuousness can veer into wry honesty. Gentle yet shaped by cooler detachment, this butterfly flight points us generously upward.

—Rohan Quine, novelist, actor and film producer

Suzi's poems represent quite a journey as they travel across a vast range of emotion and truth and yet they lighten up moments that make their subject accessible with their humour and depth.

—John Holder CBE, actor and musician

Her poetry conducts inner rhythms and vibrations. Sounds provoke visceral colour. As one reads, hope blooms, life's lustre sparks, as the page provides a canopy for spirit to flutter freely or sit quietly. She inspires the poet within.

—Wunmi Mosaku, actor

An exquisite curation. This first, magical offering sensitively picked from a lifetime's work entices you into the galaxy of Suzi's poetry. Whether you luxuriate in a single poem or fly through the volume, you will be drawn back again and again by a word that resonates or emotion reflected to re-experience Suzi's writing anew.

—Hannah Norris, actor and writer

Finally! This is a long-overdue collection of poetry by the irrepressible Suzi Rapoport. There is no one I know who has such a zest for life, and more importantly when reading this collection, so easily captures that zeal in her poetry.

—Carl Donnelly, comedian

These are small gems from Suzi's vast treasure trove of work.

—Brian Patten, poet and children's author

My sister in spirit
My lover in soul
My friend in this so solid place

—Richie Havens, singer-songwriter

Suzi—one of the most sensitive of beings.

—Hugo Manning, poet, and former poetry editor of
The New Statesman

You should have been called Oxygen not Suzi, as life always burns twice as brightly when you are around.

—Denis Apivor, composer

A poet in every sense of the word.

—Jeremy Reed, poet and novelist

Suzi is a very talented poet. An original and indelible person with a certain indefinable beauty.

—Bernard Kops, playwright, poet and novelist

A fine poet and a great person.

—Harry Landis, actor and director

Connect with Suzi Rapoport
www.suzirapoport.com

www.ingramcontent.com/pod-product-compliance
Lightning Source LLC
Chambersburg PA
CBHW030458010526
44118CB00011B/990